TRICKS AND TREATS HALLOWEEN COOKBOOK

DEDICATION

To Danny:

You've gone from little brother to playmate to friend. Although the miles may separate us, you are never truly far away.

Love you, Sis

*Danny and Valarie at Halloween
in earlier days at Presque Isle, Maine.*

Sketches by Mrs. Eugenia M. Tripp and Eric Rodenhiser

Book number: C4   © Copyright Old Saltbox 1994   ISBN 0-9626162-1-4

Printed in Canada

TABLE OF CONTENTS

CHILDREN'S COSTUME PARTY FOR 10

MENU
- Goblin Pizzas
- Berry Boo Punch
- Black Cat Sundaes
- Cat and Bat Cookies

GOBLIN PIZZAS

10 6 inch pita breads
2c your favorite pizza sauce
2c grated provolone cheese
pepperoni-thinly sliced
mushrooms-thinly sliced

1. Preheat oven to 500°.
2. Spread each pita bread with an equal amount of the pizza sauce. Top each with an equal quantity of the cheese.
3. Using a sharp knife, cut the pepperoni into squares and triangles. Allow the children to create "goblin" faces on their pizzas using the pepperoni and mushrooms.
4. Place the pizzas on ungreased cookie sheets. Bake at 500° for 5-7 minutes, or until the cheese browns. Cut in quarters with a pizza cutter or sharp knife before serving.

Serves 10.

BERRY BOO PUNCH

2 liters ginger ale
4c cranberry/raspberry juice drink
2c grapefruit juice
ice

1. In a large punch bowl, combine the cranberry/ raspberry juice drink and grapefruit juice.
2. Slowly pour in the ginger ale and stir to combine. Add ice and serve.

BLACK CAT SUNDAES

1/2 gallon chocolate ice cream
10 thin square chocolate mint candies
candy coated peanut butter pieces
black shoestring licorice

1. Cut mint candies in half to create triangles for ears. Cut licorice into short lengths for tails and whiskers.
2. To assemble sundaes, place 2 scoops ice cream in each serving bowl. Allow the children to form cats using the mint candies for ears, the peanut candies for eyes and noses and the licorice pieces for whiskers and tails. Serves 10

Keeping young children occupied and happy is a challenge for any parent. The keys are to have plenty of different activities and not to focus on any one thing for too long a time. Since children have rather short attention spans, moving from one activity or game to another is essential. This keeps everyone occupied, eliminating boredom which could lead to tears. Also, keep the party short-no more than two hours. This time frame is easier on the kids and the host! Following are some party tips that should be helpful in making your child's party a success.

1. Keep the party short-no more than two hours-especially if the children will be trick-or-treating afterward.
2. To keep the children busy while their pizzas are baking, have a "prize search". Purchase pencils, crayons, small note pads, stickers etc. at your local office supply store and hide them around a designated area of your home. The children can search for them during the time their pizzas are in the oven.
3. Give a small prize for the best pizza face. Allow Dad to judge!
4. If the party is to accompany trick-or-treats, allow the children to decorate brown paper bags to hold their candy. They could use either markers or crayons.

CAT AND BAT COOKIES

1c sugar
2/3c shortening
1 egg
1/2c sour milk
1/2t baking soda
1t vanilla
2 2/3c flour
1/2t salt

1. Preheat oven to 375°. Cut out cat or bat pattern that has been traced on parchment paper or waxed paper.
2. In a large bowl, cream the sugar and shortening. Beat in the egg ad milk, combining well. Add the dry ingredients and stir to combine.
3. Roll out dough on a lightly floured surface to a thickness of 1/8 inch. Place cookie pattern on dough ad cut out with a sharp knife. Place on a cookie sheet. Repeat with remaining dough, rerolling scraps as necessary.
4. Bake the cookies at 375° for 8-10 minutes, or until the cookies have set and are lightly browned around the edges. Remove from pan and cool on a wire rack. Makes 1-2 dozen, depending on which pattern is chosen

TEEN PARTY FOR 10 TO 15

MENU
• Turkey and Bacon Grinders
• Hot Chili
• Vegetables and Dip (recipe not included)
• Black Cat Cake
• Berry Boo Punch

TURKEY AND BACON GRINDERS

3 lb thinly sliced deli-style turkey breast
2 lb lower-salt bacon or regular bacon
16 inch sub roll per person
mayonnaise or salad dressing

1. In a large frying pan, fry the bacon one half pound at a time until crisp. Place on paper towels to drain.
2. Spread each sub roll with the mayonnaise or salad dressing. Divide the turkey and cooked bacon evenly among the rolls.
3. To serve, place the grinders under the broiler for 30-40 seconds to toast lightly. Cut in half before serving, if desired. Serves 10-15

HOT CHILI

2 16 oz cans tomato sauce
2 28 oz cans crushed tomatoes
2 16 oz cans light red kidney beans
2 16 oz cans dark red kidney beans
2 16 oz cans pinto beans
2 4 oz cans whole kernel corn

1 8 oz package cream cheese
2 packages chili seasoning
2 lb extra lean ground beef
2 large onions-thinly sliced
garlic powder to taste
crushed red pepper to taste

1. In a large frying pan, cook the ground beef and onion until browned. Drain fat and place in a dutch oven or large saucepan.
2. Add remaining ingredients and stir to combine. Simmer until all ingredients are heated through, 5-10 minutes. Serve hot with additional crushed red pepper if desired. Serves 10-15 generously

BLACK CAT CAKE

1 package your favorite white cake mix
1/2c sour cream
1 package your favorite white chocolate frosting
6 chocolate sandwich cookies
black shoestring licorice black rope licorice
orange food coloring

1. Preheat oven to 350°. Lightly grease and flour a 13x9 inch rectangular baking pan.
2. Prepare cake mix as package directs, folding in the cream cheese and adding the orange food coloring until desired shade is reached. Bake as package directs. Turn cake out onto wire rack and cool completely.
3. Place cake on serving platter and frost. Smooth frosting on top of cake using a metal spatula dipped in warm water.
4. To decorate, use the rope licorice to create a fence on the lower third of the cake, cutting short pieces to form the fence posts. Form the cats by placing the chocolate sandwich cookies on the top rail of the fence, using two cookies per cat. Using the shoestring licorice, form loops for tails and eyes. Serves 20

What do you do with teens that are too old for trick-or-treating but still want to have fun on Halloween? Here are a few ideas.
1. Have a jack-o-lantern carving contest. The for mistake proof carving are included in this book. Be sure to give a small prize to the winner.
2. Is there an artist in the group? Try face painting using acrylic paints-it will wash off with hot soap and water. The kids could chose from designs such as witches, ghosts or bats.
3. Rent age appropriate movies suited for the holiday .

HALLOWEEN MASQUERADE FOR 30

MENU
- Sweet And Sour Meatballs
- Shrimp Wrapped in Puff Pastry
- Dilled Cucumber Rounds
- Skewered Tricolor Tortellini
- Wine
- Pineapple Cheese Spread
- Brownie Triangles With Whipped Cream And Fruit

- Asparagus Stuffed Eggs
- Chicken Tartlets
- Cheese Millefoile
- Hot Crab Dip
- Coffee

SWEET AND SOUR MEATBALLS

2 lb extra lean ground beef
1 medium onion-minced
2 eggs
2t ground ginger
1/4c soy sauce
pepper to taste
SAUCE
2c sugar
1/2c vinegar
1t salt
1c water
1T catsup
1t ground ginger
2T soy sauce
1T corn starch
1/2c water
8 oz cans pineapple chunks-drained
1 4 oz jar maraschino cherries-drained

1. In a large bowl, combine the ground beef, onion, eggs, ginger, soy and pepper. Mix well. Form into 1 inch balls. Place in a large frying pan and brown on all sides.-Continue cooking 5-7 minutes, or until the meatballs are cooked through.
2. Meanwhile, prepare the sauce by combining the sugar, vinegar, salt, 1c water, catsup, ginger and soy sauce in a medium saucepan. Bring to a boil, stirring constantly.-Dissolve the 1T corn starch in the 1/2c water and add to the sugar mixture. Bring to the boil and cook one minute, or until the mixture thickens and turns clear. Stir in the pineapple and cherries.
3. To serve, pour sauce over the meatballs and place in a chafing dish or crock pot set the lowest setting. Serve warm. Serves 30

SHRIMP WRAPPED IN PUFF PASTRY

4 lb large (12-15 per pound) cooked shrimp-peeled and deveined
1 package frozen ready to use puff pastry-thawed
2T each fresh parsley and basil-minced

1. Preheat oven to 400°. Lightly oil a baking sheet.
2. On a lightly floured surface, unfold the puff pastry,-pressing together any seams that have separated. Using a crimp-cut sealer or sharp knife, cut the pastry into 60 strips 2 inches long and 1/4 inch wide, reserving any remaining pastry for another use. Wrap a pastry strip around the middle of each shrimp. Place on the prepared cookie sheet and sprinkle with the chopped basil and parsley.
3. Bake the shrimp at 400° for 5-7 minutes, or until the shrimp are pink and the pastry is puffed and golden brown Remove from the cookie sheet and cool slightly before serving. Serve warm. Serves 30

DILLED CUCUMBER ROUNDS

4 European or seedless cucumbers.
1 8 oz package soft cream cheese
2T fresh dill-minced
fresh dill sprigs for garnish

1. Wash the cucumbers under cold water. Using a sharp knife, slice the cukes into rounds about 1/4 inch thick, leaving the peel onto make them easier to pick up. Place on a serving platter
2. In a small bowl, combine the cream cheese and dill, mixing well to incorporate the herb. Place the cheese mixture in a pastry bag fitted with a #70 leaf tip
3. To assemble, pipe a leaf on each cucumber round and garnish with a fresh dill sprig. Refrigerate until serving. Serves 30

Dilled
Cucumber Rounds
ready to serve.

SKEWERED TRICOLOR TORTELLINI

2 packages fresh or 1 package dry tricolored cheese-filled tortellini
1 8 oz can black olives-drained
1 8 oz jar green olives-drained
1/2c extra virgin olive oil
1/4c balsamic vinegar or white wine vinegar
1T each fresh oregano, sage and basil-finely chopped
1 small onion-minced salt and pepper to taste
6 inch wooden skewers

1. In a large sauce pan, cook the tortellini in lightly salted boiling water until tender. Drain and place in a large, nonmetal bowl. Add remaining ingredients and toss to combine. Cover and refrigerate over night
2. To assemble, thread the pasta and olives alternately on the skewers and place on a serving tray. Serve cold. Serves 30 generously

ASPARAGUS STUFFED EGGS

2 dozen eggs-hard cooked
1 lb fresh asparagus or 1 package frozen asparagus
2 shallots-minced
mayonnaise or salad dressing
salt and pepper to taste

1. Peel the eggs under running water and slice in half lengthwise, reserving the yolks. Cook the asparagus just until tender. Drain and plunge into ice water to stop the cooking. Cut of the tips of the spears and set aside
2. Place the asparagus stalks in the bowl of a food processor along with the shallots and reserved yolks.-Process until smooth. Place the yolk mixture into a medium bowl and add enough mayonnaise to make a soft mixture, about 1/4c. Place the mixture into a pastry bag fitted with a #199 open star tip.
3. To assemble, pipe the yolk mixture into the whites and top several with the reserved asparagus tips. Refrigerate until serving. Serves 30-35

CHICKEN TARTLETS

2c cooked chicken-diced
2 shallots-minced
1/4c celery-minced
1/4c carrots-minced
1/2c mayonnaise
1t fresh oregano-minced
salt and pepper to taste
48 slices fresh bread
butter
oregano leaves for garnish-if desired

1. Preheat oven to 375°. Using a round cookie cutter, cut one circle out of each slice of bread. Lightly butter both sides and place in the muffin cups. Bake at 375° until golden brown, 5-7 minutes. Remove from the pans and cool completely
2. Combine the remaining ingredients and spoon into the bread cups. Garnish with the fresh oregano and refrigerate until serving. Serves 30

PINEAPPLE CHEESE BALL

1 8 oz package cream cheese
1 4 oz can crushed pineapple-drained and reserving
2T liquid 1 green bell pepper-minced
1/2c walnuts-finely chopped
1. In a medium bowl, combine the cheese, pineapple, pepper and the reserved juice. Stir to combine well. Refrigerate 1 hour
2. Form the cheese mixture into a ball and roll in the chopped nuts, coating well on all sides. Refrigerate until serving. Accompany with crackers or crusty bread. Serves 30

CHEESE MILLIFOILE

1 package(2 sheets) frozen puff pastry-thawed
1/2c sharp cheddar cheese-grated
1 egg yolk
1/4c milk

1. Preheat oven to 400°. On a lightly floured surface, roll out the pastry, pressing together any creases. Join the two sheets on one log edge and reroll to seal
2. Sprinkle half the cheese over the middle third of the pastry. Fold over the left third as if folding a letter.-Sprinkle the remaining cheese over the folded section and fold the right third over all. Roll out slightly
3. Using a sharp knife or pizza cutter, cut the pastry into rectangles 1x2 inches and place on a cookie sheet. Combine the egg and milk and brush on the tops of the pastry. Bake at 400° for 10 minutes, or until the pastry is puffed and golden brown. Serve hot. Serves 30
NOTE: This freezes very well and can be made weeks in advance. To reheat, place frozen in a plastic bag in the microwave for 1-2 minutes on high power

HOT CRAB DIP

3 8 oz cans crab meat
3 8 oz packages cream cheese
1/4c mayonnaise
1/3c cream cheese
1T fresh parsley-finely chopped
1 small onion-minced
1/4c parmesan cheese-grated

1. Preheat oven to 350°
2. In a large bowl, beat the cream cheese, mayonnaise and sour cream. Fold in the crab, onion and parsley. Place in a baking/serving dish and top with the grated parmesan
3. Bake at 350° for 30 minutes. Serve immediately with crackers or slices of crusty bread. Serves 30

BROWNIE TRIANGLES WITH WHIPPED CREAM AND FRUIT

2 packages your favorite fudge brownie mix
1c non-dairy whipped topping
1t orange extract segments from 2 oranges-cut into thirds
fresh mint leaves for garnish

1. Preheat oven to 350°. Grease two 13x9 inch baking pans
2. Prepare and bake brownie mixes as packages direct. When cool, cut each batch into 20 squares, then cut the squares it 4 triangles
3. In a small bowl, combine the whipped topping and orange extract. Place in a pastry bag fitted with a #16 open star tip
4. To assemble the desserts, pipe a star or ruffle design on each triangle and top with a piece of orange and a mint leaf. Refrigerate until serving. Serves 30
VARIATIONS: Using the orange cream, garnish with grated orange rind and finely chopped walnuts, or using plain cream, garnish with a strawberry slice and chocolate mint leaves. Also try flavoring the cream with 1t coconut extract and garnishing with toasted coconut.

Planning and hosting a large party can sometimes be a little frightening. I can recall a few times that I have planned a large gathering and then wished I had not!-Thankfully, there are some ways to make a big party seem less harrowing. Following are some of the things that I have learned over the years that make party time an enjoyable time for me, as well as my guests
1. Make a day-by-day list of the chores needed to be accomplished, (including cleaning!) and check off as completed. I post mine on the door of the refrigerator
2. Plan several items that can be prepared well in advance and frozen. For example, the brownies and the cheese millefiole can be bakes 2 weeks ahead and frozen until the day of the event
3. If refrigerator storage space is a problem, place less fragile items in plastic bags with zipper closings. Also stack assembled hors d'oeuvres in disposable trays. If the weather is cold, the back porch can be used as an "auxiliary refrigerator"
4. Set aside serving dishes and utensils a week in advance. Clean all silver etc. at that time. Plan your centerpiece two weeks in advance and order if necessary. If you are making your centerpiece yourself, prepare it the day before so that the flowers can refresh themselves in the container
5. Do not try a new dish for the first time at the party.-Practice it before hand for the family and get their feedback.
6. As you assemble the food, taste test everything. If you are on a diet, your spouse will love this job-mine sure does!
7. Try to have every thing prepared and ready to set out at least one hour before your guests will arrive. This will give you a few moments to relax and change into a fancy outfit without feeling rushed ENJOY YOUR PARTY!

AUTUMNAL DINNER PARTY FOR 4

MENU
• Asparagus Vinaigrette
• Ham Stuffed Chicken Breasts
• Mushroom Risotto
• Lemon Parfaits

ASPARAGUS VINAIGRETTE

1 bunch fresh asparagus
1/4c extra virgin olive oil
2T balsamic vinegar
1t fresh sage-minced
salt and pepper to taste
sage leaves for garnish, if desired

1. Steam the asparagus over boiling water until just tender, about 5 minutes. Remove from heat and chill 4 hours
2. Combine the remaining ingredients and beat with a wire whisk to create an emulsion. Divide the asparagus evenly among four serving plates and pour the vinaigrette over the base of the spears. Garnish with sage leaves. Serve immediately. Serves 4

HAM STUFFED CHICKEN BREASTS

4 boneless, skinless chicken breasts
4 thin slices proscuitto ham or honey baked ham
4 thin slices provolone cheese
2 packages ready to use crescent rolls

1. Preheat oven to 350°. Line a 13x9 inch baking dish with foil for easier clean up
2. Pound out the breasts to a thickness of 1/4 inch. Top with the ham and cheese and roll out jelly roll fashion
3. Place in the prepared pan, seam side down and bake for 1 hour or until the juices run clear. Remove from pan and chill 3 hours
4. Preheat oven to 400°. On a lightly floured surface, roll out the crescent roll pastry, pressing the sheets together to form a larger one. Cut the pastry into 4 squares. Wrap around the chicken rolls and place in a 13x9 inch baking dish. Bake at 400° for 10-15 minutes, or until the chicken is heated through and the pastry has puffed and browned. Serve immediately.-Serves 4

13

MUSHROOM RISOTTO

1/2c shitake mushrooms
3/4c arborio rice
1 clove garlic
2T olive oil
2c chicken stock
1c grated parmesan cheese
1T butter or margarine

1. In a medium sauce pan, cook the mushrooms and rice in the hot oil until the rice is translucent, stirring constantly. Add the garlic clove and the stock, cover and simmer 20 minutes, stirring occasionally. The rice mush not become dry
2. When the rice is tender but still creamy, add the butter and cheese. Remove from heat and stir to incorporate.-Serve hot. Serves 4

LEMON PARFAITS

1c graham cracker crumbs
1 package instant lemon pudding
2c nondairy whipped topping
fresh mint leaves for garnish, if desired
1. Prepare pudding as package directs. Fold in the whipped topping. Refrigerate 3 hours
2. To assemble, layer the pudding and graham cracker crumbs in parfait glasses or other attractive glasses, beginning and ending with pudding. Garnish with mint, if desired.-Refrigerate until serving. Serves 4

HOW TO CARVE A JACK-O-LANTERN

you will need:
1 nicely shaped pumpkin
sharp knife
metal spoon
pen or marker
newspaper
1 votive candle

1. If working inside, cover a large area of the floor with newspaper. Assemble tools.
2. Cut the top off the pumpkin, cutting a small notch to make replacing the lid easier. Using the spoon, scrape the seeds and stringy flesh off the lid.
3. Scoop out all the seeds and stringy flesh from the cavity of the pumpkin (kids like to use their hands) and discard. Try to scrape a small indentation in the center of the cleaned cavity for the candle to rest in.
4. On the best side of the pumpkin, draw the face. Be sure to make the features large enough so that enough air will get inside for the candle to burn. Carefully cut out the features using the sharp knife.
5. Place the candle inside the pumpkin, light and replace the lid. DO NOT LEAVE BURNING JACK-O-LANTERNS UNATTENDED

Assemble all your material before beginning.

*A cleanly hollowed
out pumpkin.*

A finished masterpiece.

*Our Jack-o-Lantern
waiting to greet the
children.*

TIPS FOR A SAFE HALLOWEEN

Unfortunately, Halloween has become dangerous in many of our communities, but there are measures that we can take to make the holiday a safe one for our children.

1. Trick-or-treat only in familiar neighborhoods and only at houses with outside lights on.
2. Accompany very young children up to the door. Wait for older children in the driveway, but within sight of the house.
3. Inspect all candy before consumption. DISCARD ANY OPENED CANDY, FRUIT OR HOMEMADE TREATS SUCH AS POPCORN BALLS.
4. Make sure all costumes do not restrict vision or movement. Make sure children carry flashlights and have reflective tape on costumes.
5. Warn children not to accept rides with strangers while out trick-or-treating.
6. Insist that older children that are going out unaccompanied travel in groups.
7. For the safety of your pets, keep them inside and confined-especially cats. Even though this is probably your dog's favorite holiday (my dogs Schultz and Brandy love to bark at the doorbell), keep them away from the door.
8. When your run out of candy, turn off the outside lights. This should tell trick-or-treaters that there are no more treats!

Happy Halloween!

DECORATOR PUMPKINS

You will need:
4 miniature pumpkins
scissors
hot glue gun and glue sticks
dried flowers such as strawflowers or roses
eucalyptus
pinecones
nuts

1. Break the stems off the pumpkins. This will create a cavity for your arrangement.
2. Using the glue gun, place the dried materials on the top of the pumpkin into an arrangement that you determine to be pleasing, cutting larger items to fit if necessary. Allow the glue to set 1 hour.
3. Place your pumpkins in desired locations, out of direct sunlight. They will last about 1-2 months.

APPLE PAN DOWDY

5 tart apples-sliced
1/4c sugar
1/4c molasses
1/2t cinnamon
1/2t salt
1/2t nutmeg
1/2c hot water
1c flour
2t baking powder
1/4t salt
2T shortening
3/4c milk

1. Preheat oven to 350°.
2. In a medium sauce pan, combine apple slices sugar, molasses, spices, the 1/2t salt, and hot water. Cook over medium heat until the apples become soft.
3. In a small bowl, combine the flour, the 1/4t salt, and baking powder. Cut in the shortening until the mixture resembles coarse crumbs. Add the milk all at once and stir to combine.
4. Place the apples in a baking dish and spoon the dough on top. Bake at 350° for 35 minutes or until the crust is puffed and golden brown. Serve warm with vanilla ice cream. Serves 4-6

ISLAND APPLE COBBLER

5c tart apples-peeled and sliced
3/4c sugar or to taste
2T flour
1/2t cinnamon
1/4t salt
1t vanilla
1/4c water
1T butter or margarine

BATTER
1/2c flour
1/2c sugar
1/2t baking powder
1/4t salt
2T butter or margarine-melted
1 egg

1. Preheat oven to 375°.
2. In a medium bowl, combine apples, 3/4c sugar, 2T flour, cinnamon, 1/4t salt, vanilla and water. Place in a 9x9 inch baking dish and dot with the butter.
3. Combine all batter ingredients and beat by hand until smooth. Drop batter in 7-8 dollops on the apple mixture, spacing evenly.
4. Bake at 375 for 35-40 minutes, or until the apples are fork tender and the crust is golden brown. Serve warm with whipped cream or vanilla ice cream. Serves 6-8

APPLE DUMPLINGS

2c sugar   3c flour
2c water   1 1/2t salt
1/4t cinnamon   3t baking powder
1/4t nutmeg   1 1/3c shortening
1/4c butter or margarine   3/4c milk
6 golden delicious apples-peeled and cored

1. Preheat oven to 375°.
2. In a medium sauce pan, combine sugar, water , cinnamon, and nutmeg. Simmer 5 minutes, remove from heat and add the butter. Set aside to cool slightly.

19

3. In a large bowl, combine the flour, baking powder and salt. Cut in the flour until the mixture resembles coarse crumbs. Add the milk all at once and stir just until moistened.

4. Turn dough out onto lightly floured surface and roll out to a rectangle 1/4 inch thick. Cut into 6 squares. Place an apple on each square and enclose with the dough. Place in a large non-stick baking pan. Spoon apple mixture around the dumplings.

5. Bake at 375° for 35- 40 minutes. Serve warm with whipped cream or vanilla ice cream. Serves 6

100 YEAR OLD PUMPKIN PIE

1 nine inch pie shell-unbaked
3/4c sugar
1/4c maple syrup
1/4t salt
1/2t ginger
1/2c cooked pumpkin
2 eggs
1/2t cinnamon
2c milk

1. Preheat oven to 375°.

2. In a medium bowl, beat the egg whites until stiff peaks form. Set aside. In another bowl, combine the remaining ingredients. Fold in the egg whites until just mixed. Pour into prepared pie shell.

3. Bake at 375° for one hour or until the center is set. Cool completely. To serve, spread with whipped cream, if desired. Serves 8-10

SPICY PUMPKIN PIE

1 nine inch pie shell-unbaked
1T butter or margarine-melted
1 1/2c cooked pumpkin
1t ginger
1t cinnamon
1/4t mace
1/4t cloves
2 eggs
2T flour
1/2c brown sugar
1//2c sugar
1/2t salt
1c milk
1t vanilla

1. Preheat oven to 450°.
2. In a small bowl, combine the pumpkin, butter and spices. Set aside. In another
bowl, beat the eggs until foamy. Stir in the flour, sugar, brown sugar, slat, vanilla
and milk. Add the pumpkin mixture and blend well. Pour filling into prepared
pie shell.
3. Bake at 450° for 15 minutes, reduce temperature to 375° and continue baking
for another 45 minutes, or until the tip of a knife inserted in the center comes
out clean. Cool completely before serving. Serves 8-10

SWEET CRUST APPLE PIE

2 3/4c flour
1c shortening
1t salt
1t baking powder
2T sugar
1 egg-slightly beaten
2T milk

FILLING

10 McIntosh apples
1/2c raisins
1/2c sugar
1 1/2t cinnamon
2T cornstarch

1. Preheat oven to 400°.
2. Combine all filling ingredients. Set aside.
3. In a large bowl, combine the flour, salt, baking powder and sugar. Cut in the shortening until the mixture resembles coarse crumbs. Add the egg and milk; stir to form a dough. Turn out on a surface that has been dusted with sugar and form into a ball; divide the dough in half. Roll out one portion and place into a 9 inch pie plate.
4. Place filling into bottom crust. Roll out remaining dough and place on top of the filing. Trim excess dough to within one inch of the edge of the pan. Fold under and crimp well. Form 3-4 steam holes by piercing the center of the top crust with a sharp knife. Brush entire top lightly with milk.
5. Bake at 400° for 10 minutes, reduce the temperature to 350° and continue baking for an additional 35 to 40 minutes. If the crust becomes too brown during baking, cover loosely with foil. Serve warm or cold with ice cream or cheddar cheese. Serves 8-10

APPLE CRUMB COFFEE CAKE

1/4c warm water-(105-115 degrees)
1 package or 1T active dry yeast
1/4c butter or margarine
1/2c sugar
1/2t salt
3 eggs
1/4c milk
2 1/3c flour

TOPPING

2-3 large apples
2/3c sugar
1/2c flour
2t cinnamon
6T butter or margarine

1. Place water into a small bowl. Add the yeast and stir to dissolve; set aside. Grease a 9x9 inch pan.
2. To prepare filling, peel, core and slice apples and place in a medium bowl. Add remaining filling ingredients and stir to coat apples. Set aside.
3. In a large bowl, cream the butter. Add the sugar and salt and cream again. Add the yeast mixture, eggs and milk and beat until well blended. Gradually add the flour, beating constantly.
4. Spread batter into prepared pan and arrange topping over all. Cover with plastic wrap and let rise in a warm place until doubled in bulk, about 1 hour.
5. Bake in a preheated 375° oven for 35-40 minutes. Cool completely before slicing. Serve slightly warm with coffee or tea.

PUMPKIN DATE BREAD

1 2/3c sugar
2/3c oil
1t vanilla
4 eggs
2c pumpkin
3c flour
2t baking soda
1 1/2t cinnamon
3/4t salt
1/2t baking powder
1/4t cloves
1c dates-chopped
1c pecans-chopped

1. Preheat oven to 350°. Grease two loaf pans.
2. In a large bowl, combine the sugar, oil, vanilla eggs and pumpkin. Add the remaining ingredients, except dates and blend just until the dry ingredients are moistened. Fold in the dates.
3. Spoon batter into prepared pans. Bake at 350° for 50 to 60 minutes or until a toothpick inserted in the center comes out clean. Cool in pans 10 minutes. Loosen bread from sides of the pans and turn out onto a wire rack. Cool completely before serving. Serve spread with cream cheese. Makes 2 loaves.

CREAM CHEESE PUMPKIN SPICE PIE

1 c sugar
3T flour
12 oz cream cheese-softened
1t cinnamon
1/2t nutmeg
1/4t ginger
1/2t cloves
3 eggs
2c pumpkin
1T milk

CRUST
1 1/2c graham cracker crumbs
3T melted butter or margarine
3T flour

1. Preheat oven to 375°. Combine all crust ingredients. Press firmly into bottom and sides of a pie pan, forming an even surface. Bake at 375° for 12 minutes or until lightly browned. Remove form oven and cool completely.
2. To prepare filling, in a large bowl, beat the sugar, flour and cream cheese until smooth;reserve 1 cup. Add remaining ingredients except milk to the remaining cream cheese mixture. Beat until smooth. Pour into cooled crust.
3. Stir milk into reserved cream cheese mixture. Spoon over pumpkin mixture. Cut through the cream cheese mixture with a knife or spatula to form swirls. Cover edge of crust with aluminum foil to prevent excess browning during baking (remove during last 15 minutes of cooking).
Bake at 375° for 35 to 40 minutes or until the filling is setand a knife inserted in the center comes out clean. Cool completely before serving. Store in the refrigerator. Serves 8

PUMPKIN ROLL

3 eggs
1c sugar
2/3c pumpkin
3/4c flour
1/2t ginger
1t baking powder
2t cinnamon
1/2t cloves
1c walnuts-chopped

FILLING
1c powdered sugar
8oz cream cheese
1/4c butter or margarine
1/2t vanilla
1c non-dairy whipped topping

1. Preheat oven to 375°. Grease a jelly roll pan, line with waxed paper and grease and flour.
2. In a large bowl, beat the eggs until thick and lemon colored. Gradually beat in the sugar, then stir in the pumpkin. Add the remaining ingredients except the walnuts and gently fold to combine. Spread batter into prepared pan;top with the nuts. Bake at 375° for 15 minutes.
3. Turn cake out onto a clean towel. Dust with powdered sugar and roll as for jelly roll, using the towel to assist you. Cool completely.
4. Prepare filling by combining all filling ingredients and beating until smooth. To assemble the Roll, gently unroll cake and spread with the prepared filling. Reroll and chill thoroughly. Dust with additional powdered sugar before serving, if desired. Store in the refrigerator. Serves 12-15

APPLE CREAM PIE

1 9 inch pie shell-unbaked
2/3c sugar
2T flour
1/8t salt
1c sour cream
1 egg
1t vanilla
2c apples-chopped

TOPPING
1/3c flour
1/3c sugar
1t cinnamon
1/4t nutmeg
1/4c butter or margarine

1. Preheat oven to 425°.
2. Prepare topping by combining the flour, cinnamon, sugar and nutmeg. Cut in the butter until the mixture resembles oatmeal. Set aside.
3. In a medium bowl, combine the sugar, flour and salt. Add the sour cream, egg and vanilla and beat until smooth. Add the chopped apples. Pour into pie shell and top with the prepared crumb topping. Bake at 425° for 25-30 minutes or until a knife inserted in the center comes out clean. Store in the refrigerator. Serves 12.

APPLE SAUCE SPICE RING

1/2c butter or margarine
1 1/2c sugar
2t cinnamon
1/2t nutmeg
1t cloves
1/2c milk
3/4c apple sauce
2t baking powder
1/4t salt
3 eggs
1c flour
1/2c currants
1 raisins
1/2c golden raisins
1c walnuts-chopped
1c rolled oats

1. Preheat oven to 350°. Grease and flour tube pan or bundt pan.
2. In a large bowl, cream the sugar and butter until light and fluffy. Add the eggs, one at a time, beating well after each addition. Add the flour, spices and milk and apple sauce, blending well. Fold in the remaining ingredients.
3. Pour batter into prepared pan. Bake at 350° for 50-55 minutes or until a knife inserted in the center comes out clean. Turn out onto wire rack and cool completely before slicing. Serves 20

APPLE CRISP

6 large, tart apples-peeled and cored
1/2c butter or margarine
1/4t nutmeg
1/2t cinnamon
1/4t salt
1/3c flour
1c sugar

1.Preheat oven to 400°.
2. Thinly slice the apples and place in a baking dish. Be sure to choose a dish large enough so that any juice formed during cooking does not boil over.
3. Combine the butter, sugar, salt, nutmeg flour and cinnamon. Cut in the butter until well combined. Sprinkle over the apples.
4. Bake at 400° for 20 minutes or until the apples are tender and the juices boil. Serve warm with vanilla ice cream whipped cream or milk. Serves 4-6

APPLE BROWNIES

1/2c butter or margarine
1 egg
1/2c pecans-chopped
1c flour
1/2t baking powder
1/4t salt
1c sugar
2 medium apples-peeled and chopped fine
1/2t baking soda
1t cinnamon

1. Preheat oven to 350°. Grease and flour a 9x9 inch pan.
2. In a medium bowl, cream the butter and sugar. Add the egg and beat well. Add the flour, baking powder, baking soda and salt and stir just until the dry ingredients are moistened. Fold in the apples and nuts. Spoon batter into prepared pan.
3. Bake at 400° for 40-45 minutes or until a knife inserted in the center comes out clean. Cool completely before slicing. Makes approximately 16 squares.

CHOCOLATE APPLE SAUCE CAKE

1/2c butter or margarine-melted
2 eggs
2c flour
1/2t cinnamon
1c raisins
1/2t salt
1c applesauce
1 1/2c brown sugar
1t baking soda
1t nutmeg
1c cocoa
red and green candied cherries

1. Preheat oven to 350°. Grease and flour a loaf pan.
2. In a large bowl, combine the butter, applesauce and eggs. Add the sugar, flour, baking soda, cinnamon, nutmeg, salt and cocoaand blend. Stir in the raisins. Turn out into prepared pan.
3. Bake at 350° for 15 minutes. Dot with the candied cherries and continue baking for another 35-40 minutes, or until a knife inserted in the center comes out clean. Turn out onto wire rack and cool completely before slicing. Makes 1 loaf.

APPLE SAUCE RAISIN BREAD

1 egg
1c apple sauce
4T butter-melted
1/2c sugar
2 1/2c flour
2t baking powder
1/2t baking soda
3/4t cinnamon
1/4t nutmeg
1c raisins
3/4c walnuts-chopped

1. Preheat oven to 350°. Grease a loaf pan.
2. In a large bowl, combine the egg, apple sauce and butter; blend well. Stir in the sugar. Add remaining ingredients, except the raisins and nuts, and blend until the dry ingredients are moistened. Fold i the raisins and nuts.
3. Pour batter into prepared pan. Bake at 350° for 55-60 minutes, or until a knife inserted in the center comes out clean. Refrigerate over night before slicing. Makes 1 loaf

PUMPKIN BREAD

4 eggs
1c oil
3c sugar
2t baking soda
1t cinnamon
2c pumpkin
2/3c water
3 1/3c flour
1 1/2t salt
1t nutmeg

1. Preheat oven to 350°. Grease three loaf pans.
2. In a large bowl, beat the eggs 1 minute. Beat in the pumpkin, oil and water. Add the sugar one cup at a time. Add the dry ingredients and mix well. Divide the batter evenly among the prepared pans.
3. Bake at 350° for one hour, or until a knife inserted in the center comes out clean. Cool completely before slicing. Makes 3 loaves
VARIATION: 2c currants or 1/12c chopped pecans may be added along with the dry ingredients. Bake as directed.

APPLE CORN BREAD

3/4c cornmeal
3/4c flour
3T baking powder
1 1/2T sugar
1/2t salt
1 egg
3/4c milk
2T oil
3/4c apple-diced fine

1. Preheat oven to 375°. Grease a 9x9 inch pan.
2. In a medium bowl, combine the dry ingredients. Add the milk and egg and stir just until smooth. Add the oil and apples and blend.
3. Pour batter into prepared pan. Bake at 375° for 20 minutes, or until a knife inserted in the center comes out clean. Serve warm with spread with butter.
Serves 6-8

FROZEN PUMPKIN PIE

1 ready-to-use graham cracker crust
1 pint vanilla ice cream-softened
1c pumpkin
1c sugar
1/4t salt
1/4t ginger
1/4t nutmeg
1c non-dairy whipped topping

1. Place the ice cream in the graham cracker crust and chill until firm.
2. In a medium bowl, combine the pumpkin, sugar,ginger, nutmeg and salt. Fold in the whipped topping and spread over the ice cream layer. Freeze. To serve, allow to sit at room temperature 5 minutes before slicing. Sprinkle each serving with graham cracker crumbs, if desired. Serves 8-10